Kingdom of Piland Chronicles

By

Ashok Malhotra

Kingdom of Piland Chronicles

© 2017 by Ashok Malhotra

Website: **https://www.facebook.com/PilandKingdom**

By CreateSpace

ISBN-13: 978-1977643414 , ISBN-10: 1977643418

Note: These chronicles contain images of documents retrieved from archives in the best available conditions but some of them do not have as good a resolution as the author would have liked. Nevertheless they have been included for record.

Chronicles

<table>
<tr><td>Contents</td><td>Page</td></tr>
</table>

July 16, 2014

The Kingdom of Piland is an experiment to test if the International principle of creation of new countries on Terra Nullius by claim, a principle by which many new countries were created in the past, is still valid in the modern world. The idea was sparked by a similar attempt recently for creation of the Kingdom of North Sudan by an American citizen. According to the proclamation of King Emperor of Piland, any citizen of the world may regard himself or herself as an adjunct citizen of this new kingdom if he or she so desires. Perhaps because of a treaty for the region, countries have not claimed this area but it seems the treaty does not apply to individuals. **Any claim made or assertion in this document or elsewhere, as regards the Kingdom of Piland, that is contrary to any international law or a national law of a nation in which it is made is to be regarded as null and void.**

A new Kingdom is born – Piland

An account of the Kingdom as first published in July 2014 at:

https://ashokmalhotra.wordpress.com/2014/07/16/a-new-kingdom-is-born-piland/

Today, I was fascinated by a news report that an American has claimed a piece of the planet that apparently belonged to no country i.e. it was Terra Nullius. He has named it the Kingdom of North Sudan and declared himself as king. I do not have sufficient knowledge of International law to know how far this claim is valid. However just for fun and as an experiment it is decided to repeat this exercise with a new Island that emerged earlier this year in the Antarctica along with an apparently previously unclaimed sector of the Antarctica – Marie Byrd land.

The name Pi Island has been tossed around for the new island because the day of it birth 3/14 and this name inspired the name of the new Kingdom. Therefore, if not contrary to law, I claim this island, including it in this Kingdom of Piland, a new country that includes Marie Byrd Land and islands in that sector off the coast of Marie Byrd Land declaring myself as the King and Emperor of Piland. Presently the population primarily consists of visiting Penguins but it shall eventually, hopefully, become a constitutional monarchy on the lines of UK with a written constitution in future. Until then proclamations of the King shall be law.

By this proclamation dated the 16th of July 2014, We the King Emperor declare Tsaven of :-

https://www.blogger.com/profile/02361550958689286343

as the Duke of the Piland Island, i.e the newly emerged island, this honor being bestowed on him due to his revealing the island to the world at

http://frozennerd.blogspot.in/2014/03/a-new-island-is-born.html subject to his acceptance of this honor.

Marie Byrd Land is the portion of **West Antarctica** lying east of the **Ross Ice Shelf** and the **Ross Sea** and south of the **Pacific Ocean**, extending eastward approximately to a line between the head of the Ross Ice Shelf and **Eights Coast**. It stretches between 158°W and 103°24'W. The inclusion of the area between the **Rockefeller Plateau** and Eights Coast is based upon the leading role of Rear Admiral **Richard E. Byrd** in the exploration of this area. The name was originally applied by Admiral Byrd in 1929, in honor of his wife, to the northwestern part of the area, the part that was explored in that year (from Wikipedia) .

All citizens of the world are regarded as adjunct citizens of the Kingdom of Piland, if they so desire, and may visit freely without visa or restriction live or visit the Kingdom of Piland if they wish, provided they do not carry out any activity to damage the environment in any substantial way and do not hurt or kill any plant, animal or fish beyond what is required for their short term food, clothing or shelter needs. – By Proclamation of the King Emperor of the Kingdom of Piland, the creation of the Kingdom is an attempt to protect this portion of the planet from any unnecessary exploitation aside from an exploration of new innovative laws and practices.

The primary goal of creation of the Kingdom of Piland is to make contributions towards protecting and enhancing the environment of the planet.

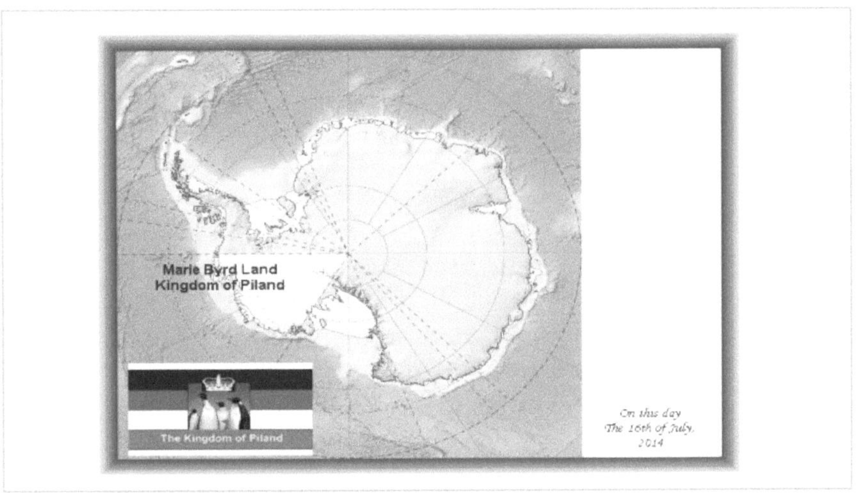

Marie Byrd Land in Antartica, image from (modified before use here)
**http://commons.wikimedia.org/wiki/File:Marie_Byrd_Land_in_Antarctica_%28
Relief%29.svg**
This file is licensed under the Creative Commons Attribution-Share Alike 3.0
Unported license.

You may claim citizenship (or as associate in case your country does not permit dual citizenship) to this new as yet experimental country (an experiment in International law) on facebook merely by liking the page at

https://www.facebook.com/PilandKingdom

NOTE: Please register any sound objections, if any, that you may have to the idea of Kingdom of Piland as described as a comment. If you do not, this Kingdom will become a reality.

It goes without saying that as long as there is no fairly permanent human settlement and habitation in the Kingdom of Piland by persons who regard themselves as its citizens, the Kingdom must remain a merely symbolic thing or at best a first step only. Yet it is not impossible that an unexpected turn of events would make such a settlement possible. It would then become a physical reality.

This appears to be similar to "New Jersey v. New York, 523 US 767 (1998)". US Supreme Court. May 1998. Retrieved 29 January 2010.

"Even as to terra nullius, like a volcanic island or territory abandoned by its former sovereign, a claimant by right as against all others has more to do than planting a flag or rearing a monument. Since the 19th century the most generous settled view has been that discovery accompanied by symbolic acts give no more than "an inchoate title, an option, as against other states, to consolidate the first steps by proceeding to effective occupation within a reasonable time.8 I. Brownlie, Principles of Public International Law 146 (4th ed.1990); see also 1 C. Hyde, International Law 329 (rev.2d ed.1945); 1 L. Oppenheim International Law §§222-223, pp. 439-441 (H. Lauterpacht 5th ed.1937); Hall A Treatise on International Law, at 102-103; 1 J. Moore, International Law 258 (1906); R. Phillimore, International Law 273 (2d ed. 1871); E. Vattel, Law of Nations, §208, p. 99 (J. Chitty 6th Am. ed. 1844)."

Governance

July 16, 2014

Through a note on Facebook His Majesty the King of Piland stated that at an appropriate time if the Kingdom gets established the Kingdom of Piland shall have a system of Governance similar to UK by default wherever explicit differences are not stated but with some essential differences. There shall be no political parties and no election, as in the original democracy at Athens, so that love and harmony can be maximized between for all. A House of Commons will be selected by random selection when citizens increase. The PM and leader of house of commons too similarly and they can be changed by members at any time by a constructive vote of Ayes and No's. There shall also be a House of Lords. Until such time as these houses are constituted the Kingdom shall function with proclamations of his Majesty.

This idea of democracy through random selection developed in the mind of His Majesty by observing the state of democracies as exist around the world in present times. His Majesty has expressed his philosophical views on this elsewhere in a note entitled Spirituality and Democracy elsewhere. It is reproduced here for record

Democracy and Spirituality

Democracy is a form of government in which people through a vote choose representatives to govern them for defined periods, except in a few African states where glue appears to stick democratically elected leaders to their seats of power forever, metaphorically speaking. The precise form of democracy varies from country to country. Most have a written constitution that describes principles through which a state is governed. In many cases, though not all, democracies have produced greater welfare of people than other forms of government such as dictatorships, or monarchies.

However, democracies as exists in most countries today are not free of defects, some serious. This brief note cannot go into various advantages and defects of democratic forms of government but it may be mentioned that the biggest short comings of democracies arise from the role of money in elections and later in law making so that people often end up with laws that favor big money interests rather than them. It is as the root of much misery in the modern world ranging from wars, financial crisis to homelessness. Modern democracies have produced a huge number of slick smooth talking politicians who say the right thing for votes and go on to do the wrong thing to line their pockets and secure a seat of power for their dirty bums. The greater the level of hypocrisy the more successful the politician.

Our life is pushed in directions that are the source of our focus. It is because of this that Saints advice that we most focus on good and good humans and try to draw our mind away from any evil that exists in others, leaving the universe to deal with it, for the most part. However, democratic elections are not like that. A contest between opposing candidates leads to focusing on the weaknesses and evil if any in opponents and shouting about it over the roof tops. This involves all of the adult population of a nation and as per spiritual understanding this may lead to compromising not just the character of a nation as a whole but the very soul that dwells within. However such a sling fest appears unavoidable in modern forms of democracies because for a nation to thrive it is essential that democratic elections pick up those with good moral character and exposes to throw out those with poor one, because as said in an ancient highly revered spiritual work from South Asia,

Original and future possibilities for democracies

Democracy today arose from the ancient Athens idea of democracy. We know that Athenians had created a highly evolved form of human civilization. However they had avoided the problem of money interests as well as character assassinations when they chose their representatives by choosing their representatives for brief periods, simply at random, from names thrown in a pot and picked up as lottery numbers. In modern times a set of hundred or five hundred names can similarly be picked up from all interested citizens through a computer or even better a combination of both, a computer for a short list of a few thousand and then a manual process like the lotto so that none could say the selection was rigged by a computer. Perhaps a minimum age limit of 30 or 40 may be set for representatives after further debate. Some countries may wish to add a minimum qualification of a high school pass so that deliberations are literate by all members. A brief educational course may be organized for chosen persons to familiarize them with procedures. This will take governments out of hands of greedy pigs, wheeler-dealers and glib talkers who have perfected the art of saying the right thing for votes and doing the wrong thing to line their pockets. Just as rapists are attracted to where beautiful women live, robbers and criminals attracted to where treasure is stored, often the worst of society is attracted to where power and money lie. It is not surprising therefore that many such ends up as representatives of people in modern democracies.

The feeling of this author is that this last proposal similar to the original Greek democracy would lead to a sounder and better House of Commons or representatives than exist today. However, there would be a limitation in such a congress. The majority can often run rough shod over interests of a minorities and this house would tend to do that. Further more educated and evolved levels of government are required to prevent that or any other decision that may be taken due to a temporary emotional upsurge, something similar to an upper house of parliament.

An upper house of parliament can similarly be picked up by random selection, say hundred persons from a list of the thousand most educated persons in a nation. The most educated are defined as a thousand with the highest educational degrees held for the longest periods since graduation. This thousand would change by the time the next election comes around. It would change rapidly, if an upper age limit of say 75 years were set for lawmakers and this upper house would consist of experienced older highly educated persons and intellectuals of the nation, certainly a wiser selection than the present House of Lords of UK.

Random selections of upper house and lower house in such a democracy will make it highly unlikely for lawmakers to win a second term and thus chances of getting corrupted by power will be far less than lawmakers who hang on for decades. it shall truly be a representative government. Some financial incentive and awards may be instituted for law makers that perform well based on a public poll at the end of term

Prime Minister and President

The question some ask is in such a party less system how shall a Prime Minister and President be chosen. An existence of political parties is not necessary for democracies to function and may in fact be detrimental. Such leaders can be chosen in the lower house and upper house respectively by a majority vote. Successive rounds of voting would be required if there are several nominees to discover the popular choice. Once appointed such leaders may be changed only by a constructive no-confidence vote i.e. where a new replacement is simultaneously voted on. Votes on legislation would be based on the conscience of each member and not by party considerations.

At every stage of development humans think they have reached the highest possible stage of development in the universe, whether it is with economic models such as capitalism or communism, models of governance, medicine, spiritual knowledge, science or what have you. Ignorant humans push the idea further. The truth is that the universe is infinite and evolution through it infinite. Humans shall continue to evolve; periodically falling every time they attain a degree of progress and prosperity because then greed shall raise its ugly head. Nothing blinds humans more than an upsurge of greed, lust and anger leading them to their downfall.

How The Idea of Kingdom of Piland was born

The idea of Kingdom of Piland was inspired by an article in the Washington Post at a similar attempt a little earlier, through which the Kingdom of North Sudan was established,

https://www.washingtonpost.com/news/morning-mix/wp/2014/07/15/this-virginia-man-founded-kingdom-of-north-sudan-but-jeopardy-champ-ken-jennings-suggested-it-first/?tid=hp_mm&utm_term=.2544be4d9001

The report states that a Virginian man, Jermiah Heaton stated that:

"Today, I planted this flag in the Eastern African region of Bir Tawil to honor a promise I made to my daughter," Jeremiah Heaton **decreed**. "Therefore, so be it proclaimed on June 16, 2014, Emily's 7th birthday, that Bir Tawil shall be forever known as the Kingdom of North Sudan. The Kingdom is established as a sovereign monarchy with myself as the head of state; with Emily becoming an actual Princess. … Long live the Kingdom."

The report goes on to state that,

In today's heavily mapped globe, Bir Tawil is a very unusual spit of land and there **are few like it.** The legal name for such unclaimed places is, **according to international law**, terra nullius: "land that belongs to no one." And "It conveys a concept that a sovereign state can acquire any unoccupied or unsettled land. Some but not all scholars **contend** European colonials frequently employed it to claim new lands, sealing the deal with physical objects such as coins and flags. "Historically, staking a physical claim is the first rule of the discovery doctrine," **explained** Robert J. Miller of the Lewis & Clark Law School."

About Marie Byrd Island

According to Wikipedia at
https://en.wikipedia.org/wiki/Marie_Byrd_Land

Marie Byrd Land is the portion of **West Antarctica** lying east of the **Ross Ice Shelf** and the **Ross Sea** and south of the **Pacific Ocean**, extending eastward approximately to a line between the head of the Ross Ice Shelf and **Eights Coast**. It stretches between 158°W and 103°24'W. The inclusion of the area between the **Rockefeller Plateau** and Eights Coast is based upon the leading role of Rear Admiral **Richard E. Byrd** in the exploration of this area. The name was originally applied by Admiral Byrd in 1929, in honor of his wife, to the northwestern part of the area, the part that was explored in that year.

Because of its remoteness, even by Antarctic standards, most of Marie Byrd Land (the portion east of 150°W) has not been claimed by any sovereign nation. It is by far the largest single unclaimed territory on Earth, with an area of 1,610,000 km² (620,000 sq mi) (including Eights Coast, immediately east of Marie Byrd Land).

Five coastal areas are distinguished listed from East to West

No.	Sector	Western Border	Eastern Border
1	Saunders Coast	158°00'W	146°31'W
2	Ruppert Coast	146°31'W	136°50'W
3	Hobbs Coast	136°50'W	127°35'W
4	Bakutis Coast	127°35'W	114°12'W
5	Walgreen Coast	114°12'W	103°24'W
	Marie Byrd Land	**158°00'W**	**103°24'W**

Proclamation of His Majesty, the King of Piland

July 17, 2014

The citizenship of the Kingdom of Piland has begun to grow. Welcome to all the new citizens. Who knows that some day this might become a real country that all of you would be the proud founding citizens of. If not, you would still be proud of having been the proud citizens of this icy yet marvelous part of our planet - The Antarctica - even for a while.

A few have worried, what would happen if they become citizens of a new country if they belong to one that does not allow dual citizenship, in case the Kingdom of Piland becomes a recognized country. To safeguard your current citizenship, the Kingdom of Piland has promulgated a new law as of this moment - that all such citizens belonging to countries that do not permit dual citizenship with the Kingdom of Piland - shall be only prospective citizens, until such time as this dual citizenship is permitted. However, prospective citizens shall have all rights as equal to full citizens.

With this now the different categories of citizens of the Kingdom are

1. Prospective/provisional citizens
2. Adjunct citizens which are all and any citizen of the world who so desires

All categories of citizens may visit/live without visa or restriction in the Kingdom of Piland to carry any activity that they desire which is not destructive to plants, animals and environment of the Kingdom except whatever is necessary for their immediate needs of food, clothing and shelter in the Kingdom. In this respect the idea of the Kingdom of Piland protects at least one part of our planet, howsoever remote from environmental damage.

Authorized by His Majesty, the King Emperor, **Kingdom of Piland**

A Dukedom for Sir Hugh Ashton

July 17th, 2014

An announcement of the Facbook page of the Kingdom today said,

Hugh Ashton, welcome to the Kingdom of Piland. A letter patents has been issued by the King Emperor that grants you Knighthood and the Dukedom of Carney Island off the coast of Marie Byrd Land. This in recognition of your contributions to modern language and literature and knowledge of foreign lands. Henceforth you shall be known as Sir Hugh Ashton, Duke of Carney. Please Read about your icy realm here

http://en.wikipedia.org/wiki/Carney_Island

Know Ye all by these Presents, that by the Authority invested in Us, We do hereby, in Recognition of his Knowledge of Strange Lands and their Peoples, and his Achievements in Language and Literature, Hugh Ashton, a resident of Japan, is henceforth to be recognised and styled as Duke of the Island known as Carney Island, located at 73° 57'S 121° 00'W and that this Island, with the Emoluments and Perquisites thereby pertaining, shall be the exclusive Demesene and Dominion of the said Hugh Ashton.

Subject to restrictions as placed His Royal Majesty from time to time

Given under our Hand and Seal, this, the Eighteenth Day of July in the Year Two Thousand and Fourteen:

King Emperor of Piland, Aclob the First
The House of Nambu

For the His Imperial and Royal Majesty the King Emperor of Piland

Kingdom of Piland –Protecting the Planet

Published on July 16, 2014 at
https://someitemshave.blogspot.in/2014/07/kingdom-of-piland-
protecting-planet.html

It has been mentioned in various places that mankind needs to do more to protect our environment and forests. While different parts of the world have been under the jurisdiction of different countries of the world and the responsibility falls upon them, surprisingly there were still a couple of areas that were Terra Nullius, at least until a few weeks ago. Aside from protecting the environment, it would also be good if different countries use the area under their control to help at least some others such as refugees fleeing their countries under severe distress or violence and much has been written about that in recent posts.

The two new countries have now been declared as two new Kingdoms, the Kingdom of North Sudan and the Kingdom of Piland. The first is a very tiny desert area and the second an icy sector of the Antarctica. It is not known if these claims would stand the test of time since they are very new. However, either they will or someone else will claim them or perhaps they shall be placed as a common heritage of mankind. Fortunately the second, the Kingdom of Piland has already done that in a way. It has declared that any citizen of the world may regard himself or herself as an adjunct citizen and live/visit this Kingdom provided they do not undertake any activity that damages the plants, animals and environment of the region, and that is the message of this new Kingdom for the entire planet too.

The primary objective in the creation of the Kingdom of Piland is to make contributions towards protection of the planet from environmental degradation aside from the fun of a nearly out of the world, almost fictional adventure.

His Majesty further stated that,
It must be mentioned that others have claimed parts of the Kingdom of Piland in the past but none of the claims have been recognized by any other nation so far. Therefore it appears that officially it is still Terra Nullius. This is just one more attempt. Perhaps this one will gain recognition, because its aim is for all of the world rather than individual benefit. Worth a try in any case

The Royal Seal
July 18, 2014

The Royal Seal, Designed by Sir Hugh Ashton, Duke of Carney. The seal is used in all important documents by his Imperial and Royal Majesty, King Emperor Ashok the First of the House of Nando,

Baroness Angelique Matos of Hannah

Know Ye all by these Presents, that by the Authority invested in Us, We do hereby, in Recognition of her Knowledge of Philosophical traditions originating in the Himalayas combined with a modern knowledge of Finace, Angeliue Matos a Resident of New York is henceforth to be recognized and styled as the Baroness of Hannah, Pertaining to the Island of Hannah located at Coordinates: 76 39'S 148 48'W

Given under our Hand and Seal, this, the Eighteenth Day of July in the Year Two Thousand and Fourteen:

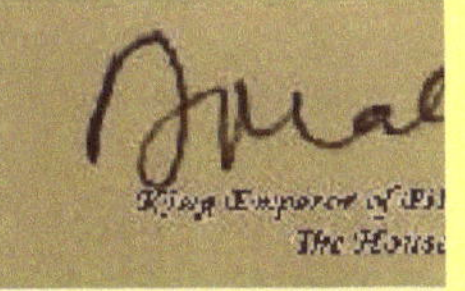

For the His Imperial and Royal Majesty the King Emperor of Piland

Earl Ricardo Alexander (Ricky Gomez)

Know Ye all by these Presents, that by the Authority invested in Us, We do hereby,

declare that Ricardo Alexander (also known as Ricky Gomez)

resident of Florida is henceforth to be recognised as the Earl of of the Island known as Benton Island, located at Coordinates: 77 ᵒ S 147 33 W the title having a status and recognition that is no more or no less that the status of the Kingdom of Piland

Given under our Hand and Seal, this, the twentieth day of July in the Year Two Thousand and Fourteen:

Royal seal and signature

For His Imperial and Royal Majesty the King Emperor of Piland Ashok the first of the house of Nando

Shining Light of the World
July 20, 2014

President Jose Mujica of Uruguay has been chosen as the Shining Light of the World, for the year 2014 as a Birthday Honor by His Imperial and Royal Majesty the King Emperor of Piland.

His Majesty has been a great admirer of President Jose Mujica as an exemplary President in the modern Democratic world. He has written a note about him elsewhere that is repeated here for record.

Jose Mujica the godly President

While democracy has spread across the world, many politicians are not regarded very highly by the population at large in several countries. Several are seen as working for their own interests or to protect the interests of a vested minority and sing the song of the one percent.

However on this scene there is a clear exception. He is Jose Mujica, the President of Uruguay, a politician who is loved by his people. José Mujica has been President of Uruguay since 2010. Mujica was born on 20 May 1935 to Demetrio of Basque Spanish ancestry and Lucy, a daughter of Italian immigrants. Mujica's father was a small farmer who faced bankruptcy.

At a time when many world leaders impose austerity on their citizens, Mujica himself maintains a simple and austere lifestyle. He has been described as the world's poorest president due to his austere lifestyle. Yet in his heart he regards himself as the richest and most fortunate of human beings. The joy of this content shines brilliantly on his face. He says,

"I'm called 'the poorest president', but I don't feel poor. Poor people are those who only work to try to keep an expensive lifestyle, and always want more and more,"

True enough how can one measure riches by wealth alone? A poor person is one who wants, not one who gives. The richest is the one who gives away most of his income most of the time. He refused to live in the Presidential Palace, but instead lives on his wife's simple farm on the outskirts of Montevideo where he and his wife grow and sell fruits and flowers. He drives an old 1987 VW beetle. He donates 90% of his Presidential salary to charity. He's a citizen like any other, except he doesn't have a bank account. Mujica's annual salary is about US$ 150,000 but he keeps only 10% of it for personal expenses and transfers the rest to a Foundation which supports small productive enterprises and NGOs working on housing developments for the poor. Mujica offered the use of the official presidential residence to serve as shelter for homeless families. He dresses casually like an ordinary farmer most times but is not averse to wearing a suit and tie if the occasion demands. Needless to say it is gentle humanity and joy that is written all over his countenance rather than sleaze and misery often found on the faces of many other politicians along with a sulk and a frown.

Under his mandate, Uruguay has prospered economically and socially to become one of the most paradise like countries on the planet. He is a socialist but is not averse to capitalism when it helps everyone rather than just a few. The unemployment rate in Uruguay is lower than that of the US.

Many of his views on God and religion are similar to those of Buddha except that he does not regard life as suffering but as something beautiful worth cherishing and an opportunity to contribute joy to the world. He neither affirms God nor denies Him, regarding the entire Universe, all of nature and all life within it as a manifestation of a Universal consciousness. Needless to say he is a vegetarian but in an informal Lovegan way like Buddha not in a fanatical vegan way. It is a view of spirituality that is similar to a view of spirituality as portrayed in this blog. In his own words:

"Every day I believe a little bit more in Nature. I learned this very simple lesson: life is beautiful so you have to live it with intensity and pursue happiness."

In June 2012, his government made a move to legalize state-controlled sales of marijuana in order to fight illegal drug trade and the misery it causes. Time magazine featured an article on the matter. Mujica said that by regulating marijuana business, the state will take it away from drug traffickers, and weaken the drug cartels. The state would also be able to keep track of all marijuana consumers in the country, and provide treatment to the most serious abusers, much like what is done with alcoholics. There is an older post on **Cannabis** in this blog that describes how keeping cannabis illegal is harming humanity rather than helping it although it does create a profit for criminals and others who feed on that profit that includes officials and politicians. As a result, instead of killing each other in huge numbers and ending up with a corrupt police force as in Mexico and other countries, under the project 'war on drugs', Urguayans are loving and kissing each other instead, while psychiatric sickness and drug related crime common in many other countries is fast disappearing from the land. The contribution of cannabis to improve psychiatric health has been discussed in detail in this blog at the earlier link on cannabis. A side benefit is that alcohol related deaths from road accidents have also come down because some of the people now smoke hash instead which appears to be less addictive than tobacco and kills fewer people than alcohol.

Uruguay, under the leadership of one enlightened leader based in love and truth, Jose Mujica won the war on drugs with love, not guns while in other countries such as Mexico they are still busy killing each other over it.

More recently, moved by compassion and concern, he volunteered to take some Guantanamo Bay prisoners in his country. Therefore here is one person, a President, one can not but help classify as a saint or godly. He does not belong to the present but to a future when the world moves away from the rule of hypocrisy and one percent to a rule that caters to the interests of the majority while protecting interests of minorities. Currently, the world has yet to move out of even one person rule in all of the countries of the world. It was not too long ago that the world was ruled by kings and queens and therefore it does not see absurdities of amazing concentrations of wealth and/or power in a few hands while others are homeless or starve. Needless to say the more it is the rule of one person in reality, the more it is either ordained by God or the peoples rule in lying words and descriptions. Atrocious lies are the handmaiden of oppression and the devil, just as love, truth and simplicity are those of the gentle and the godly.

Know Ye all by these Presents, that by

a study of reports, this year

President Jose Mujica of Uruguay

Has been chosen as

The Shining Light of the World

as an example of excellence for all in

his chosen field of activity

in the year two thousand and fourteen

For the His Imperial and Royal Majesty

the King Emperor of Piland

A Birthday Honor Presentation by King Emperor Ashok the First of Piland

Currency of Piland

July 19, 2014: His Imperial and Royal Majesty has issued one side of the design concept for a 500 Piland Dollar coin. Being cast in fine gold, it shall need no control by any central bank and no recognition anywhere. it shall have value in all the realms and regions of the world because of the gold. Its value with respect to other currencies shall fluctuate as the value of gold fluctuates, but it tends to fluctuate less than the whims of some governments of the planet in the modern era that control the printing press and may indulge in constipative easing referred politely as a quantitative one. However the owners of this currency shall not be subject to inflation because of it as are dwellers of other countries. Lower denominations shall not be issued in the first era of the Kingdom rather this single coin may be exchanged for any other permissible currency of any country for the latter use. The Tails side:

On the Heads side the coin shall be styled as the five pound Uma of 1839. The earth has been styled as the Goddess Gaia or as the goddess with the lion recognized for ten thousand years of mankind's history as the mother goddess

Due to its expected thin population, His Majesty has decided not to issue any smaller denomination of currency at the present time but rather used any other available notes and coins of other countries of the world for the purpose as announced from time to time.

A Message about Peerage to an admirer

July 20, 2014

After careful observation His Imperial and Royal Majesty, King Emperor of Piland desires to include some in the Peerage. Being a newly founded as yet unrecognized Kingdom, it goes without saying that all such titles have similar status, no greater or no less than the Kingdom of Piland itself or for similar period of time; His Imperial and Royal Majesty too would love to hold a title in the Peerage but The Sovereign is considered the fount of honor and, as "the fountain and source of all dignities cannot hold a dignity from himself"

Shannon Ann Koyle, Countess of Cruzen

Know Ye all by these Presents, that by the Authority invested in Us, We do hereby, declare that Shannon Ann Koyle

resident of Newfoundland and Labrador is henceforth to be styled and recognized as

the Countess of the Island known as Cruzen Island, located at 74 47'S 140 22'W Coordinates the status and recognition of the title being similar to the status and recognition of the Kingdom of Piland

Given under our Hand and Seal, this, the twentieth day of July in the Year Two Thousand and Fourteen:

Royal seal and signature

For His Imperial and Royal Majesty the King Emperor of Piland Ashok the first of the house of Nando

The Coat of Arms of His Majesty King Emperor Ashok of Piland

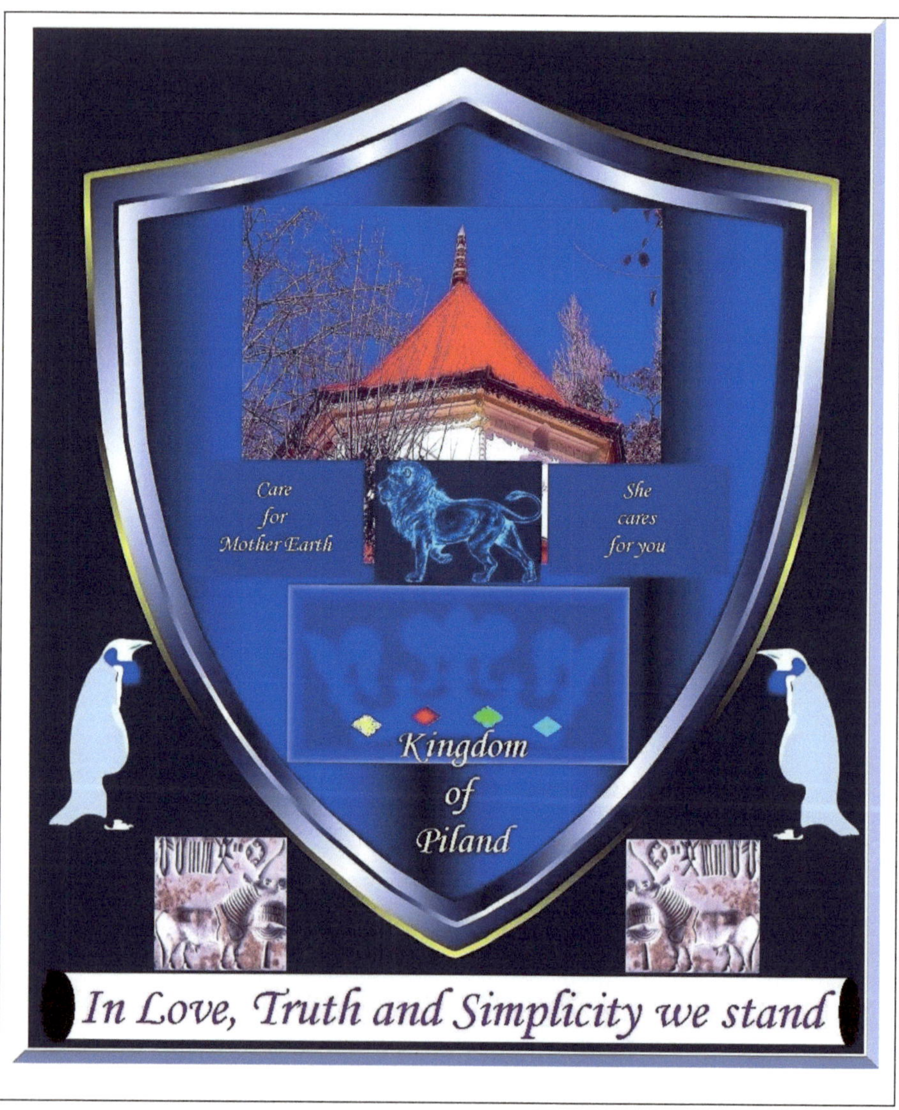

Love Not War

July 21, 2014

A visitor the Kingdom of Piland said that war would be fun and to make it possible he lays claim to the land. He was banished/blocked from the Kingdom because the Kingdom of Piland believes in Love not war as enshrined on its coin. - Love, Truth and Simplicity. A leading spiritual inspiration for his Majesty has been

https://www.facebook.com/truthsimplicityloveservice

Brad Nelson the Duke of Hobbs
July 22, 2014

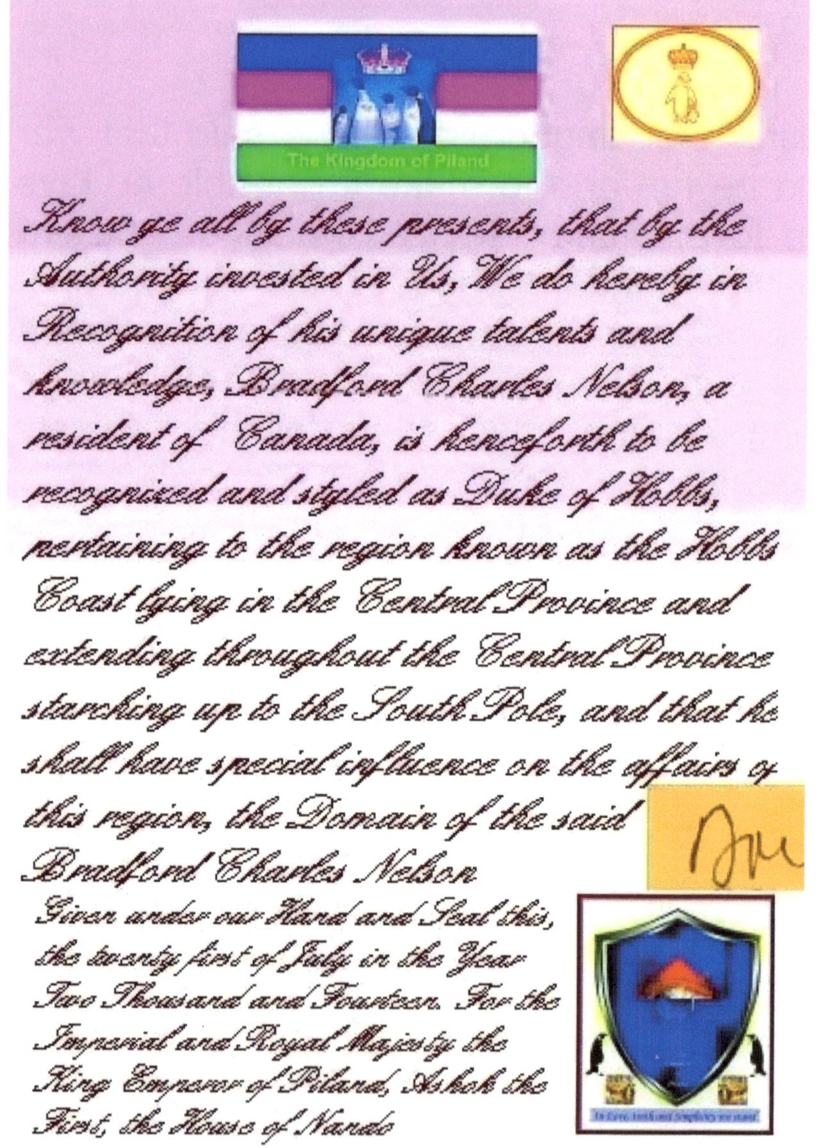

Invitation July 22, 2014

37

A Dukedom in the Kingdom is open to any former Prime Minister of New Zealand if he or she should so desires (serving ones would be too busy), that being the closest country to the Kingdom of Piland and to Prince Harry of England or any other direct descendent of Queen Victoria if it ever pleased them, up to a limit of 11 though because she had a lot of grand children, since our systems draw inspiration from UK and their most eminent Queen and Empress Victoria, with some differences for simplifications e.g. We shall not have a Marquis in the peerage for simplicity.

Himanshu Kotnala, recognized as the Count of Kramer Island by his Majesty

Know ye all by these presents, that by the Authority invested in Us,

We do hereby in Recognition of his unique efficiency and humanitarian leanings, Himanshu Kotnala, a resident of Antwerp, Belgium, is henceforth to be recognised and styled as the Count of Kramer Island (77°14'S 147°10'W). And as a member of the Peerage, he shall have special influence on the affairs of the kingdom. The status and recognition of this status is similar to that of the Kingdom.

this title is similar to that of the Kingdom

Given under Hand and Seal by His Imperial and Royal Majesty, King Emperor of Piland, Ashok the First of the House of Nando

FREEDOM OF BELIEF

July 24, 2014

His Majesty has strong spiritual beliefs but none that belong exclusively to any one religion or philosophical system. They arise from both the east and the west, from ancient beliefs as well as modern ones. However he believes strongly that every human has a right to his or her own belief or none at all, and that any fanaticism in such matters is detrimental to further evolution since no finite mind, not even saints and angels, may ever know fully the mysteries of the infinite. His majesty's views on life, spirituality, economy and environment recorded over several years can be found in the blogs

http://someitemshave.blogspot.com
https://ashokbabji.blogspot.com

Countess Angelique Matos honored as the Countess of the Guest Pennisula

The twenty seventh day of July

In the year two thousand and fourtenn

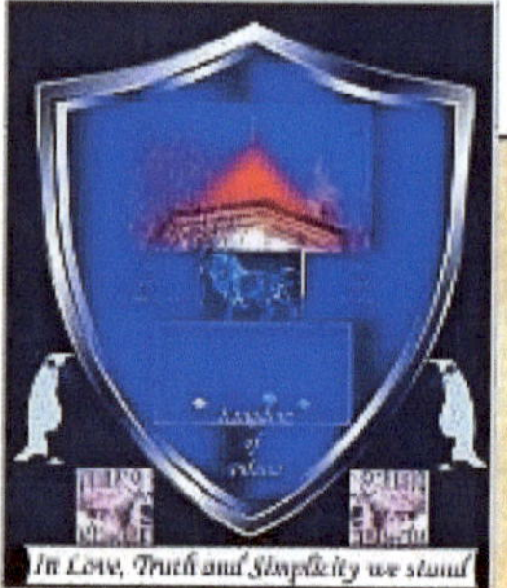

Know ye all by these presents, that by the Authority invested in Us,

We do hereby declare in Recognition of her unique and active contribution to the affairs of the Kingdom and unique efficiency that Baroness Angelique Matos, a resident of New York, is henceforth to be recognized and styled as the Countess of the Guest Pennisula. The Peninsula is a peninsula about 45 miles long between the Sulzberger Ice Shelf and Block Bay in the northwest part of Marie Byrd Land. This is in addition to her existing position in the peerage as Baroness of the nearby island of Hannah. As a member of the Peerage, she shall have special influence on the affairs of the kingdom. The status and recognition of this title is similar to that of the Kingdom.

Given under Hand and Seal by His Imperial and Royal Majesty, King Emperor of Piland, Ashok the First of the House of Nando

Sir Martin Olson the Duke of Walgreen
August 12, 2014

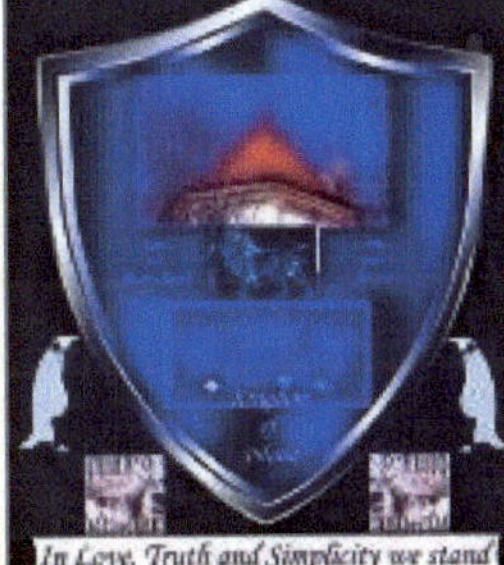

The 12 of August

In the year two thousand and fourteen

Know ye all by these presents, that by the Authority invested in Us,

We do hereby declare in Recognition of his rare creative talents and active contribution to the affairs of the Kingdom that Sir Martin Olson is henceforth to be recognized and styled as the Duke of Walgreen or the Eastern province lying in a triangular sector stretching from the Walgreen Coast (103°24'W to 114°12'W) to the Southern Pole. As a member of the Peerage, he shall have special influence on the affairs of the kingdom. The status and recognition of this title is similar to that of the Kingdom.

Given under Hand and Seal by His Imperial and Royal Majesty, King Emperor of Piland, Ashok the First of the House of Nando

A Masterpiece by Shawn Leonhardt in honor of the Kingdom of Piland, Penguins of Piland

https://soundcloud.com/shawnleonhardt/penguins-of-piland

August 18, 2014

In the year two thousand and fourteen

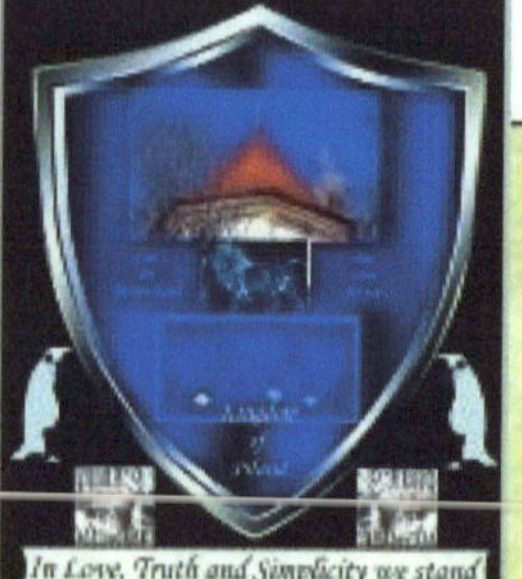

Know ye all by these presents, that by the Authority invested in Us,

We do hereby declare in Recognition of his rare talents in the creation and production of complete songs of an exotic quality and excellence and active contribution to the affairs of the Kingdom that Sir Shawn Leonhardt is henceforth to be knighted and recognized and styled as the Baron of Bandy Island (75°4'S 137°49'W Coordinates). As a member of the Peerage, he shall have special influence on the affairs of the kingdom. The status and recognition of this title is similar to that of the Kingdom.

Given under Hand and Seal by His Imperial and Royal Majesty, King Emperor of Piland, Ashok the First of the House of Nando

Legalisation of Cannbis
September 9, 2014

Countess Angeliue Matos mentioned that, "It's legal for me to take OPIODS until I'm stiff with rigor mortis to control pain from RA, but illegal for me to smoke MJ to control pain and prevent serious stomach issues. Oreos, potato chips and cellulite would be the worst I would suffer from the latter."

As a consequence, of the Countess Matos plea, His Majesty the King Emperor of Piland is hereby pleased to announce that the sale, trade, possession and consumption of Marijuana in its natural form, fresh or dried is now completely just as legal in the Kingdom of Piland as bread or lettuce is. This legality however does not cover the extracts of this plant that the drug industry tries to get into for their obscene profits and which tend to be harmful being an unnatural product. His Majesty has written much elsewhere on the legalization of cannabis and mentioned that for thousands of years cannabis was legal and created no notable problems for mankind while alcohol and opium have created problems through history. All of the modern problems of cannabis seem to have begun after it was made illegal. Keeping it illegal also diminishes modern research into its many reported benefits.

Yoga
June 10, 2015

The 21st of June is International Yoga day and the Kingdom of Piland heartily supports this day. It is a good day to introduce yoga in one's life and a good way to get ready for that is entropy yoga that His Majesty has formulated earlier and written much about elsewhere. It can be found easily through a google search. It was a result of combined scientific and mystic interests of his Majesty who has worked as a scientist for his living through much of his career. Yoga is about spiritual treasures that survive death rather than material ones that stay with us only briefly through this life. It is to unite our consciousness with its infinite source rather than only a finite mind of our present body.

His Simplicity, His Majesty
July 14, 2015

Proclamation on this day, the fourteenth of July, in the year of our Lord, two thousand, one hundred and fifteen

While the address 'Your Majesty or His Majesty' is a mark of power, grandness and awe, the address 'Your Simplicity' or 'His Simplicity' is a mark of the infinitely superior powers of Love, Truth and Simplicity. Therefore, hence forth such as those citizens, friends or members of the Kingdom of Piland who prefer to use just the latter address or none at all for the Kings and Queens of Piland, for all time to come, shall be considered delightful. It may be mentioned that the Kingdom has members and friends who belong to countries that do not permit citizenship of more than one country and the Kingdom itself has as yet no establishment of its own. Therefore such as these may regard themselves as friends and members of the Kingdom but enjoy all rights precisely equal to that of others citizens even without being one. As a matter of fact the King and Emperor of Piland, falls precisely in this latter category too. It may be mentioned that the Kingdom shall be exactly one year old on the twentieth day of July, 2015. It was announced to the world in the public domain a few days prior to that. The King sends his warm wishes of peace and happiness for all citizens, friends and members of the Kingdom

~

Countess Gilane Gullett Smith
July 14, 2015

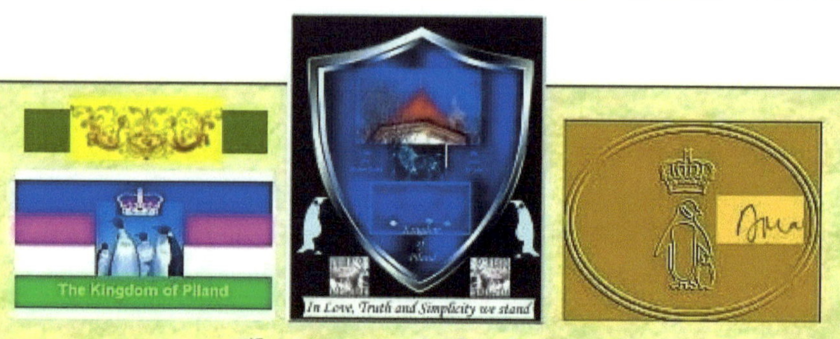

The Fourteenth of July, 2015

Know ye all by these presents, that by the Authority invested in Us,

We do hereby declare in Recognition of her rare talents and active contribution to the affairs of the Kingdom that Lady Gilane Gullett Smith is henceforth to be recognized and styled as the Countess of Brownson Islands. a group of about 20 small islands which lie just outside the entrance to Cranton Bay in the Kingdom of Piland. As a member of the Peerage, she shall have special influence on the affairs of the kingdom. The status and recognition of this title is similar to that of the Kingdom.

Given under Hand and Seal by His Simplicity, King Emperor of Piland, Ashok the First of the House of Nando

Ashok M.

Proclamation on First Anniversary of Kingdom

Kingdom of Piland

A message from His Majesty the King on the occasion of the first annual Anniversary of the Kingdom

Dear friends, citizens and dwellers of the Kingdom of Piland, heartfelt greetings and best wishes to you on the first annual anniversary of the Kingdom, the twentieth of July, 2015. By a fortunate set of circumstances this date also happens to be the Birthday of Your Majesty, the King. It was a few days before the twentieth of July 2014 that the formation of the Kingdom on a terra nullius portion of Antarctica was announced last year.

Neither all the treaties nor all the laws governing formation of Kingdoms on terra nullius in general and Antarctica in particular are known in all their detail and complexity to the King and he left it to the world at large to raise objections if any to this adventurous experiment. In the year since it was announced on blogger, wordpress and facebook, there has been no such objection. There has been a silence from the rest of the world except for one person who suggested he would love to wage a war on the Kingdom and win it from us. He was told that the Kingdom believes in peace not war and we have never heard from him since.

The experiment although based on real terra firma and with real people involved remains a virtual one so far in the sense that no physical activity has so far been carried out in the Kingdom. It is a difficult terrain, far away, and any such exercise is expensive. His Majesty, now more often referred to as His Simplicity is exploring possibilities on how to proceed in that direction. If and when such plans develop he would share it with all of you as he has shared everything to do with the Kingdom from the start.

Best wishes to all of you, your family and friends

Ashok M.

Development

January 17, 2016

Any development on the Kingdom of Piland needs a rich adventurous billionaire to invest in view of the remote cold snow covered climate of the Kingdom. Rather than wait for global warming to do it, His Majesty would be delighted if there is a billionaire out there who shall invest and put up a resort a location of his choice in the Kingdom in a manner that causes no damage to the pristine environment of the Kingdom. In return his Majesty shall grant such a billionaire the title of Duke that can be passed on by inheritance, in the same way as hereditary titles in the UK, of that area and surrounding lands of a substantial extent, subject to the same level of recognition and restrictions if any that may exist in International law as prevails. However the selected area must not encroach upon the titles already awarded. In order to verify the seriousness of the contender, His Majesty shall request the billionaire to first make a small investment (of less than a million) elsewhere in the world at a selected location. This post may be taken as an announcement of this offer. Perhaps some billionaire would love to become a Duke

A Gift from Mother Earth

September 15, 2017

The Kingdom of Piland is a spiritual gift from mother Earth. Perhaps it is because of her Spiritual nature no material development has taken place in the Kingdom but it remains a huge source of inspiration in service of Mother Earth. May Mother Earth bless all of the friends, well wishers, citizens, Lords and Ladies of the Kingdom.